Sojourner Truth

History Maker Bios

Laura Hamilton Waxman

LERNER PUBLICATIONS COMPANY • MINNEAPOLIS

Lerner Publications Company
A division of Lerner Publishing Group, Inc.
241 First Avenue North
Minneapolis, MN 55401 U.S.A.

Website address: www.lernerbooks.com

Library of Congress Cataloging-in-Publication Data

Waxman, Laura Hamilton.
    Sojourner Truth / Laura Hamilton Waxman.
        p.   cm. — (History maker biographies)
    Includes bibliographical references and index.
    ISBN–13: 978–0–8225–7172–8 (lib. bdg. : alk. paper)
    1. Truth, Sojourner, d. 1883—Juvenile literature. 2. African American
abolitionists—Biography—Juvenile literature. 3. African American women—
Biography—Juvenile literature. 4. Abolitionists—United States—Biography—
Juvenile literature. 5. Social reformers—United States—Biography--Juvenile
literature. I. Title.
E185.97.T8W38 2008
305.5'67092—dc22 [B]   2007022993

Manufactured in the United States of America
1 2 3 4 5 6 – JR – 13 12 11 10 09 08

TABLE OF CONTENTS

Introduction

Sojourner Truth grew up as a slave in the early 1800s. She was called Isabella when she was a slave. She gained her freedom as an adult. Later on, she gave herself a new name, Sojourner Truth. Then she set out on a new life.

Sojourner knew that most black people in the United States still lived in slavery. She traveled the country speaking out for their freedom. Her deep voice and wise words inspired people to fight against slavery.

Sojourner also gave powerful speeches on behalf of women. She and other women did not have the same rights as men. Sojourner spoke out for those rights. She especially fought for women's right to vote.

This is her story.

1 A SLAVE IN NEW YORK

Isabella was born a slave in Hurley, New York. A man named Johannes Hardenbergh owned Isabella and her family. Like many slave owners, Mr. Hardenbergh did not bother to keep track of when his slaves were born. No one knows Isabella's exact birth date. But it was probably some time in 1797.

As slaves, Isabella's parents had to work for Mr. Hardenbergh without pay. James and Betsey had no freedom to leave the farm or change their lives. Worst of all, Mr. Hardenbergh could sell them or any of their children to other slave owners whenever he pleased.

Isabella's parents had eleven or twelve children. But Mr. Hardenbergh had sold nearly all of them. James and Betsey lived in fear that Isabella would be sold, too.

Any slave could be sold at any time. Many African American slave families were separated this way.

Johannes Hardenbergh died when Isabella was still a baby. His son, Charles, took over his father's property. That included his land, house, animals, and slaves. Charles moved Isabella's family out of a small cottage on the farm. Instead, he made all his slaves live in the cellar beneath his home. The cellar was cold, dark, and damp. Isabella and the other slaves slept on piles of straw. Underneath, water and mud often came up through the loose floorboards.

Many slaves such as Isabella lived in places that had no furniture.

As a slave, Isabella had to obey her owner. There was always a lot of work to do. She had little time to visit her family.

It was a hard life. But at least Isabella lived with her family. Then Charles Hardenbergh died. His family decided to sell his property. That included the black men, women, and children he owned. They sold Isabella to a man named John Neely. She was around nine years old.

Mr. Neely did not live very far away. Still, Isabella hardly ever saw her parents again. She was lonely and scared. Mr. Neely did not give her warm enough clothing for the bitter New York winter. And he punished her often with his whip.

About a year later, Isabella's luck changed. Mr. Neely sold her to another family in New York. The Schryvers were not as cruel as Mr. Neely had been. But they did not keep Isabella for long. They sold her to another family in 1810.

Isabella's new owner was John Dumont. Mr. Dumont lived in New Paltz, New York. Right away, he put thirteen-year-old Isabella to work on his farm. His wife, Sally, made her do work in the house too. Isabella had to do many extra chores such as cooking and laundry.

Dumont was a French name. Many French settlers built homes, such as this one, in New Paltz in the 1700s.

Wheat (LEFT) was a common crop in New York when Sojourner was a slave. Corn and apples grew there too.

Mr. Dumont praised Isabella for her strength. He said she could do more work than his strongest male slaves. Still, he beat or whipped her if she did anything that made him angry.

On the Dumonts' farm, Isabella grew into a slim young woman. She was almost six feet tall. She had a deep, low voice.

A man named Robert fell in love with Isabella. Robert worked as a slave on a nearby farm. He often sneaked away to visit Isabella. But Robert's owner wanted Robert to marry one of his own slaves. He ordered Robert to stop seeing Isabella.

SLAVERY IN THE NORTH

In the 1600s and 1700s, people could own slaves in both northern and southern states. By the time of Isabella's birth, many northern states had begun to outlaw slavery. By the mid-1800s, black people in all northern states were freed. But slavery remained a big part of life in the South.

Robert kept visiting Isabella anyway. One day, his owner secretly followed him to the Dumonts' farm. From her window, Isabella saw the owner attack Robert. He beat Robert nearly to death. After that, Robert never visited Isabella again.

About 1815, Isabella married a man named Thomas. Tom was also a slave on Mr. Dumonts' farm. Isabella and Tom had five children.

One of them probably died as a young child. The others were Diane, Peter, Elizabeth, and Sophia. Isabella had to care for her children and also get all her work done.

Sometimes she brought her children with her to the field. She put her youngest baby in a basket. Then she hung the basket from a tree. An older child swung the basket to help the baby sleep.

Isabella's life was the same day after day. She worked from morning until night. She earned no money. She had no freedom. Her days were a lot like her parents' had been. And it seemed like nothing would ever change. But big changes were coming.

2 TAKING HER FREEDOM

A new state law changed Isabella's life forever. The law said that slave owners in New York had to free all slaves born before July 4, 1799. That included Isabella and her husband. The law said they had to be freed by July 4, 1827. Younger slaves would get their freedom as adults. Males had to turn twenty-eight years old to be freed. Females had to be twenty-five.

John Dumont promised Isabella and Tom that he would free them a year early. He even said he would let them live in a cottage on his farm. Isabella waited and waited for that day. But by July 4, 1826, Mr. Dumont had changed his mind. He said he wasn't going to free Isabella and Tom early after all.

Isabella decided to take matters into her own hands. One fall morning, she got up just before daybreak. She tied her few belongings into a cotton handkerchief. She picked up her baby, Sophia. Then she sneaked away from John Dumont's farm.

Many slaves left their owners in groups, such as this one. Sojourner was brave to go alone.

Isabella left her other children behind with her husband. Tom did not want to leave the farm. Isabella knew she could not feed and clothe all of her children on her own. Tom promised to take care of them.

Isabella learned about a nearby white family named the Van Wagenens. Isaac and Maria Van Wagenen were abolitionists. They believed that slavery should be abolished, or outlawed. The Van Wagenens agreed to take in Isabella and Sophia. In exchange, Isabella did chores for them. But she was not their slave. She could leave them any time she wished.

Isabella was glad to have Sophia with her. But she missed her other children.

Northern slaves had many paths to freedom in the 1800s. This letter promises a slave her freedom after ten years.

Weeks later, John Dumont tracked down Isabella. He said he wanted her to return to his farm. But Isabella had made up her mind. She wasn't ever going back to slavery again. The Van Wagenens paid Mr. Dumont twenty dollars to free Isabella one year early.

Isabella was happy with her new life. But that happiness did not last long. In 1827, she learned her young son, Peter, had been sold to a Southern slave owner. Slavery had not been outlawed in the southern states. She might never see him again.

Lawmakers (ABOVE) gathered at the capitol building in Albany, New York. They passed a law that said slaves could not be sold in New York state.

Isabella knew that what happened to Peter was against the law. A New York law said that no slaves could be sold to slave owners in the South. She went to the Dumonts' farm. She asked Sally Dumont to help her get her son back. But Sally didn't care about Isabella's pain. She said nothing could be done for Peter. Isabella knew better. "I'll have my child again," she promised. She felt strong inside.

Isabella decided to take her case to court. She had never been to a courthouse or spoken to a judge. She didn't know any other black person who had done so either. But that didn't stop Isabella. She got advice from some abolitionist friends. She found two lawyers to help her for free. After many months of hard work, Peter was returned to Isabella. The court also gave him his freedom.

Isabella was in her early thirties. She wanted to make more of her life. She decided to move to New York City. Many freed black men and women went there to find work. She hoped to do the same.

More than 150,000 people lived in New York City when Isabella moved there in the late 1820s.

Isabella found jobs in people's homes doing laundry, cooking, and cleaning. Many of the families she worked for were members of the Methodist religion. She had also joined this Christian religion. She often went to church services to pray and listen to the ministers preach. At times, other church members also stood up to lead prayers and songs. Isabella became one of them.

ISABELLA'S RELIGION

Isabella's mother had taught her to pray to God whenever she was scared or sad. But Isabella did not belong to any religion as a slave. She became a Christian after she escaped slavery. Isabella's religious beliefs were important to her. She had a strong faith that God would protect her from danger. She also believed God would always lead her in the right direction. Those beliefs gave her courage to stand up for herself and others throughout her life.

Isabella also began taking part in prayer meetings around the city. At these religious gatherings, she and others preached to anyone who would listen. She inspired people with her loud, deep voice and powerful words. People began coming just to hear her. They liked the way she spoke of her Christian beliefs and her strong faith in God. She hoped her listeners would become strong Christians, too.

Isabella lived in New York City for more than ten years. She had a good life there. She could buy her own food and clothing. She even bought some new furniture. But she dreamed of something more. She wanted to make a difference.

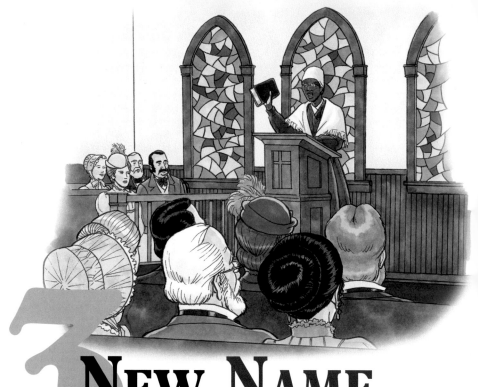

3 NEW NAME, NEW LIFE

A round the age of forty-six, Isabella decided to make a change. She was going to leave New York City. She planned to become a traveling preacher. She wanted to inspire as many people as possible with her religious beliefs and faith in God.

Isabella's plan was very unusual for the time. Many Americans believed it was improper for women or black people to speak in public. Few women were successful preachers. Even fewer black women preached or gave speeches. But that didn't stop Isabella.

She began her new life on the morning of June 1, 1843. She also gave herself a new name. She called herself Sojourner. A sojourner is a visitor who never stays in one place for long. That's how she planned to live—as a traveling preacher. Soon she gave herself a second name, Truth. She hoped to always speak the truth to others.

Juliann Jane Tillman was a preacher in the 1840s when Sojourner began to preach. But little is known about Juliann.

Sojourner Truth traveled across New York, Connecticut, and Massachusetts. She preached in churches and at outdoor religious meetings. People loved to hear her speak. They also liked the way she sang religious songs in her deep, strong voice.

Sojourner enjoyed her new life. But by winter, she needed a rest. She decided to join a new community in Northampton, Massachusetts. It was called the Northampton Association.

The Northampton Association community house

An association member sketched Sojourner doing laundry for the community.

White and black people lived and worked side by side at the Northampton Association. Together, they ran a silk factory. They sold the silk they made. Then they used the money to take care of all the community members.

People at the Northampton Association led a simple life. They hoped to make the world a better place. Many of them were abolitionists. They invited famous abolitionists to come share their ideas.

One of the most famous abolitionists was William Lloyd Garrison. He had been leading the fight to end slavery in the South. Another famous abolitionist was Frederick Douglass. Douglass, like Sojourner, had once been a slave. After he escaped slavery, he became a writer, newspaper editor, and abolitionist speaker. Both Garrison and Douglass came to the Northampton Association. Sojourner met them and listened to their ideas about ending slavery. She liked what she heard.

William Lloyd Garrison published an antislavery newspaper called the Liberator.

Frederick Douglass (SEATED TO THE RIGHT OF THE TABLE) waits to speak at an abolitionist meeting.

Sojourner also listened to community members talk about women's rights. Most people thought women should only be wives and mothers. Women were not allowed to have many kinds of jobs. They could not make laws or help lead the country. They could not vote. Women's rights supporters believed women should have the same choices as men.

Sojourner learned a lot from her friends at the Northampton Association. She was sad when it ran out of money in 1846 and had to close. Once again, she worked in people's homes to make a living. But she still dreamed of making a difference.

Sojourner Truth's True Words

In 1850, Sojourner published a book about her life. It was called *Narrative of Sojourner Truth*. It told the story of her life as a slave and as a free person. But it was not written in Sojourner's own words. She could not read or write. A friend wrote down her story for her. Other people wrote down some of Sojourner's speeches. Sometimes different people wrote the same speech in very different ways. Not everyone in modern times agrees about which words Sojourner truly spoke.

In 1850, Sojourner bought a small home of her own in Northampton. By this time, her children were free adults. Sojourner invited them to come live with her.

Around that same time, Sojourner began speaking at abolitionist meetings. There, people talked about how to end slavery in the South. Sojourner used her skills as a preacher to catch the crowd's attention. Often, she spoke about her life as a slave. Her words brought people to tears. She inspired them to keep fighting for black people's freedom.

Sojourner also spoke at many women's rights gatherings. She gave one of her most famous speeches in 1851. That year, she went to a large women's rights gathering in Akron, Ohio.

Elizabeth Cady Stanton (STANDING) was a women's rights leader. She gave speeches about women's rights as Sojourner did. Elizabeth was also one of Sojourner's friends.

In her speech, she argued that women were equal to men. She used herself as an example. Sojourner spoke about the farmwork she had done as a slave. "I have plowed and reaped and husked and chopped and mowed, and can any man do more than that?" She believed that women could work as hard as men. It was time for women to have the same rights, too.

Once a group of angry white men began hissing and shouting at her. Sojourner stayed calm. "You may hiss all you please," she said. No one could stop her from speaking the truth.

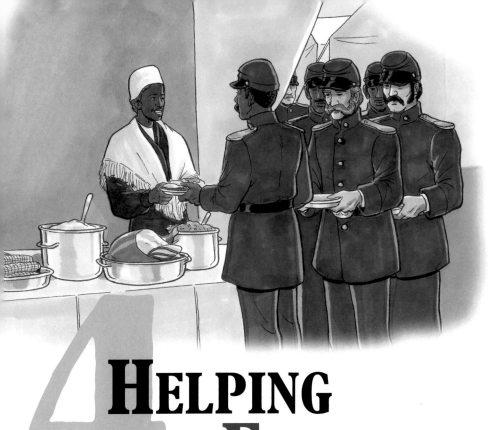

4 HELPING THE FREE

Sojourner Truth was becoming a well-known speaker for women and southern slaves. Newspaper reporters wrote articles about her. Famous abolitionists and women's rights leaders wanted to meet her. Sojourner kept giving speeches. She hoped her words would make a difference.

Around 1857, Sojourner sold her house. She moved to a small community called Harmonia. It was near Battle Creek, Michigan. Neighbors in Harmonia treated black and white people equally. Abolitionists also lived in the area.

More and more northerners believed slavery should be outlawed in the South. But southerners did not want to give up their slaves. War finally broke out between the North and the South in April 1861. It became known as the Civil War.

The Civil War began at Fort Sumter, South Carolina.

A poster asks African American men to fight for the North in the Civil War.

Sojourner was proud that one of her grandsons signed up to be a soldier in the North's army. She encouraged other black men to fight in the Civil War. She also found ways to support black soldiers.

Sojourner knew that a large group of black soldiers was training in Detroit, Michigan. In 1863, she asked people in Battle Creek to give her food for a Thanksgiving dinner. She brought the food to the soldiers in Detroit. She spoke and sang to them. She gave them courage.

African American men from the South also joined the North's army. Many of them had escaped slavery to become soldiers. Other slaves fled the South to make a new life in the free North.

Thousands of these black men, women, and children ended up in Washington, D.C., the nation's capital. Once there, they were considered to be free. But most of them had no homes or jobs. Sojourner wanted to help these escaped slaves. In 1864, she decided to go to Washington, D.C.

African American Company E fought for the North. These men are at Fort Lincoln, near Washington, D.C.

MEETING THE PRESIDENT

In 1864, Sojourner Truth (BELOW LEFT) met with President Abraham Lincoln (BELOW RIGHT), in the White House. He helped the North win the Civil War. And he worked to free African Americans from slavery. Sojourner wanted to thank him for all he had done. In later years, she also met with presidents Andrew Johnson and Ulysses S. Grant.

Former slaves stand beside tents put up by the U.S. government.

Sojourner arrived in the city in the fall. She was shocked by what she saw. The U.S. government had set up camps for the many people who had fled to the capital. Many families lived in small, rundown shacks. They did not have proper food or clothing.

Sojourner quickly got to work. She gave speeches to the former slaves. She visited them in their shacks. She encouraged them to make more of their freedom. Sojourner told them they did not have to depend on the government to survive. They could take care of themselves. They could have a better life. But most of them did not know how.

Many of them had spent their lives working in someone else's fields. They had never learned how to run a home, find a job, or save money. Sojourner had taught herself to do all these things. She told them that they could learn, too. She gave lessons on how to clean, cook, knit, and sew.

The North won the Civil War in 1865. After that, slavery was outlawed everywhere in the United States. Sojourner was thrilled. But she knew that African American families needed a lot more help to make a new start in life.

Millions of newly freed African Americans like this group had a lot to learn about freedom. Sojourner was ready to help them.

5 FIGHTING ON

After the war, Sojourner worked hard to find jobs for freed slaves. She matched black men and women with northerners who needed good workers. Sometimes she used her own money to pay for the workers' train tickets to the North.

But by 1867, Sojourner's money had run out. She had also begun to miss her home.

Sojourner sold her house in Harmonia. She moved to an old barn in Battle Creek, Michigan. She planned to fix it up into a nice home for herself and her family.

Sojourner liked being back home. But she still did not stay there for long. She often traveled across the country giving speeches.

Sojourner gave many speeches on behalf of the freed slaves. She knew they had suffered terribly under slavery. And they had not earned money for their hard work. She said they deserved to be paid back in some way.

Sojourner helped freed African Americans, such as these men, get jobs.

Sojourner shared her belief with lawmakers and other U.S. leaders. She told them that the U.S. government owed freed slaves land of their own. That would help make up for all the years the country had allowed slavery to go on. With land, black families could earn money as farmers. They could make a new start in life. Some U.S. leaders agreed with her. But the government did not follow her plan.

Ho for Kansas!

Brethren, Friends, & Fellow Citizens:
I feel thankful to inform you that the
REAL ESTATE
AND
Homestead Association,
Will Leave Here the
15th of April, 1878,
In pursuit of Homes in the Southwestern Lands of America, at Transportation Rates, cheaper than ever was known before.

For full information inquire of

Benj. Singleton, better known as old Pap,
NO. 5 NORTH FRONT STREET.
Beware of Speculators and Adventurers, as it is a dangerous thing to fall in their hands.
Nashville, Tenn., March 18, 1878.

Benjamin Singleton was a former slave. His poster invites other freed slaves to go to Kansas. In Kansas, they could get land of their own.

Sojourner was often the only African American woman to speak at women's rights gatherings.

Sojourner also made time to go to women's rights gatherings. Women's rights leaders had begun to spend most of their time fighting for the right to vote. Sojourner spoke about the right to vote, too. She also said that women should help lead the country. She believed women would make excellent lawmakers, government leaders, and judges.

As usual, Sojourner was often the only black woman to speak at these gatherings. She was also one of the only poor women's rights leaders. Most of the other women were well off. They had never needed to work to survive. They did not always think about the lives of poor women.

THE RIGHT TO VOTE

Women were not the only ones fighting for the right to vote. African American men also wanted to vote. They won that right in 1870. But many southern states found ways to keep black people from voting for the next one hundred years. Sojourner and other women's rights supporters died before they were allowed to vote. Women did not get the right to vote until 1920.

Sojourner explained that working women did not get paid the same as men. That made it much harder for them to take care of themselves and their families. She hoped women's rights supporters would fight for poor women, too.

Giving speeches about women's rights was important to Sojourner. But she believed women should act. They should reach out and take those rights for themselves.

Sojourner decided to follow her own advice. In 1872, she tried to vote in Battle Creek. Sojourner was not arrested. But she was not allowed to vote either. Still, she refused to stop fighting for that important right.

By 1880, Sojourner had begun to travel less. She was in her eighties. Her health wasn't good. But many people still wanted to hear her words and ideas. They came to visit Sojourner at her home.

Sojourner Truth died on November 26, 1883. She has not been forgotten. Her strength, courage, and ideas have set an example for people everywhere.

TIMELINE

In the year . . .

1806	the Hardenbergh family sold Isabella to John Neely.	Age 9
1808	she was sold to Martin Schryver.	
1810	she was bought by John and Sally Dumont.	
1815	she married Thomas, another slave. her first child, Diane, was born.	Age 18
1821	her son Peter was born.	
1825	her daughter Elizabeth was born.	
1826	her last child, Sophia, was born. she escaped slavery in the fall.	Age 29
1829	she moved to New York City.	
1843	she became a traveling preacher on June 1. she changed her name from Isabella to Sojourner Truth.	
1844	she joined the Northampton Association.	Age 47
1850	she published *Narrative of Sojourner Truth.* she began speaking at abolitionist and women's rights meetings.	
1851	she gave one of her most famous speeches.	Age 54
1861	the Civil War began.	
1864	she went to Washington, D.C., to help freed slaves. she met with President Lincoln on October 29.	
1865	the Civil War ended. slavery was outlawed throughout the United States.	Age 67
1867	she returned home to Michigan.	
1883	she died on November 26 at the age of 86.	

REMEMBERING SOJOURNER TRUTH

Sojourner Truth is remembered for her inspiring words and actions. People have found many ways to honor her in modern times. Here are just a few examples.

- Sojourner Truth was added to the National Women's Hall of Fame in 1981. It is in Seneca Falls, New York.

- The U.S. Postal Service printed stamps with Sojourner Truth's picture on them in 1986.

- In 1996, the National Aeronautics and Space Administration (NASA) named a rover *Sojourner*, after Sojourner Truth. The rover was a six-wheeled robot that explored land on Mars two hundred years after Sojourner Truth was born.

- The Sojourner Truth Institute was formed in Battle Creek about two hundred years after her birth. The institute is dedicated to honoring Sojourner's life.

- In 1999, a twelve-foot-tall statue was added to a park in Battle Creek. It is known as the Sojourner Truth Monument.

The Mars rover Sojourner explored the planet.

45

FURTHER READING

Bial, Raymond. *The Strength of These Arms: Life in the Slave Quarters.* Boston: Houghton Mifflin, 1997. Learn what daily life for slaves in the South was like.

Clinton, Catherine. *Hold the Flag High.* New York: Katherine Tegen Books/Amistad, 2005. Discover the true story of a skillful group of black soldiers and their black leader fighting for the North during the Civil War.

Landau, Elaine. *The Abolitionist Movement.* New York: Children's Press, 2004. Landau presents a history of the fight to outlaw slavery throughout the United States.

McPherson, Stephanie Sammartino. *Susan B. Anthony.* Minneapolis: Lerner Publications Company, 2006. This is a biography of the famous women's rights leader and her fight to give women the vote.

Poulakidas, Georgene. *The Civil War.* New York: Powerkids Press, 2005. This book provides short history of the war that ended slavery in the United States.

Welch, Catherine A. *Frederick Douglass.* Minneapolis: Lerner Publications Company, 2003. Welch presents a biography of this famous black abolitionist and leader.

WEBSITES

Pathfinder Rover Gets Its Name
http://mpfwww.jpl.nasa.gov/rover/name.html This website explains how the name Sojourner was chosen for the Mars rover.

The Sojourner Truth Institute
http://www.sojournertruth.org This organization's website includes information about Sojourner's life and times as well as a "Test Your Knowledge" quiz.

SELECT BIBLIOGRAPHY

Bernard, Jacqueline. *Journey Toward Freedom: The Story of Sojourner Truth.* New York: Feminist Press at the City University of New York, 1990. First published 1967 by W. W. Norton & Co.

Fitch, Suzanne Pullon, and Roseann M. Mandziuk. *Sojourner Truth as Orator: Wit, Story, and Song.* Westport, CT: Greenwood Press, 1997.

Mabee, Carlton, and Susan Mabee Newhouse. *Sojourner Truth: Slave, Prophet, Legend.* New York: New York University Press, 1993.

Olive, Gilbert. *Narrative of Sojourner Truth.* New York: Oxford University Press, 1991.

Painter, Nell Irvin. *Sojourner Truth: A Life, A Symbol.* New York: W. W. Norton & Co., 1996.

Sojourner Truth in Ulster Country
http://www.newpaltz.edu/sojourner_truth

Stetson, Erlene, and Linda David. *Glorying in Tribulation: The Life Work of Sojourner Truth.* East Lansing, MI: Michigan State University Press, 1994.

INDEX

Acknowledgments

For photographs and artwork: The images in this book are used with the permission of: © MPI/Stringer/Hulton Archive/Getty Images, pp. 4, 41; © North Wind Picture Archives, pp. 7, 8, 9, 16, 39; Library of Congress, pp. 10 (HABS NY, 56-NEWP, 4-2), 23 (LC-USZC4-4543), 26, 32 (LC-USZC4-528), 34 (LC-DIG-cwpb-04294), 35 (LC-USZ62-16225), 37 (LC-DIG-cwpb-01005); © Brand X Pictures, p. 11; © Theodor Kaufmann/The Bridgeman Art Library/Getty Images, p. 15; Manuscripts, Archives & Rare Books Division, Schomburg Center for Research in Black Culture, The New York Public Library, Astor, Lenox and Tilden Foundations, p. 17; © CORBIS, p. 18; © Museum of the City of New York/CORBIS, p. 19; Historic Northampton, Northampton, Massachusetts, pp. 24, 25; Madison County Historical Society, Oneida, New York, p. 27; © Bettmann/CORBIS, pp. 29, 39; © Kean Collection/Staff/Hulton Archive/Getty Images, p. 33; © Time Life Pictures/Stringer/ Getty Images, p. 36; © The Granger Collection, New York, p. 40; courtesy of NASA, p. 45. Front cover: © Bettmann/CORBIS. Back cover: Library of Congress (LC-DIG-ppmsca-08979).
For quoted material: pp. 18, 30, Gilbert Olive, *Narrative of Sojourner Truth* (New York: Oxford University Press, 1991). First published in 1878 in Battle Creek, MI, for the author; p. 30 (second paragraph), Nell Irvin Painter, *Sojourner Truth: A Life, a Symbol* (New York: W. W. Norton & Co., 1996).